Living Well in

Froggy's World

of Plenty

Sweet Talk to
Read Aloud

Living Well in Froggy's World of Plenty

Sweet Talk to Read Aloud

Judith Ellison Shenouda

Shenouda Associates Inc.
Pittsford, NY, USA

First Edition 2017
Second Edition 2018

Creative design and editorial services by Shenouda Associates Inc.

Photo of author by Lauren Muldoon

Shenouda Associates Inc.
Pittsford, NY, USA

ISBN-13: 978-1-7322223-0-4
ISBN-10: 1732222304

Contents

Preface

Most years have 365 days, but 2016, with 366 days, was a leap year. On February 29, the day that was added, *look before you leap*, *leaps and bounds*, *a quantum leap*, *leaping lizards*, *leap frog*, and more words came to mind throughout the day. *Leap of faith* lingered longer than the other leaps.

That's when a little story about Froggy started to poke into consciousness. Through him and his many critter friends, I wanted to explore the concepts of healing and wellness and figure out how physical, emotional, and social annoyances can dissipate and even disappear.

While writing the short, flash stories in this book, I ensconced myself in a happy place that was free of warts, a metaphor for life's irritation. By writing about and living in Froggy's perfect world of plenty, I began to see that imagining, focusing on, and experiencing the good, the healthy, and the positive can have miraculous results. With light and laughter, sweetness and sustenance, work and hobbies, and prayers and praises, our world of plenty becomes a joyous, healing place.

Because much of my professional work involves writing technical manuals that are precise, concise, and constrained in terms of word choice, *Living Well in Froggy's World of Plenty* allowed me the license to have fun with words.

I hope the many word plays, even the corny and absurd, offer a healing chuckle. While the words, the stories, and the book will have greater meaning for adults, children, too, can benefit, especially if the sweet talk is read aloud to them.

This second edition starts with a Preface and concludes with Reflections to ponder. Answering the questions helps to make meaning of Froggy's world, allowing you to apply the many bits of wisdom to your world.

While this book explores living well in nature, the living well theme finds a place in my other books.

Career Success in 12 Easy Steps: A Journal serves as a guide to living well at work.

A Bisl of This, A Bisl of That: Eating Our Way has recipes and stories for living well with food, family, and friends.

My wish is that these books help you find ways for living well— in nature, at work, and with food, family, and friends.

Dedication

May 28, 2017

Happy 100th birthday, my precious, much loved mother, Gertrude Shulman Ellison, my Ma. How you relished a party, gathering family and friends into our Euclid home where we ate, we laughed, we sweet talked, we played, and we sang along with you at the piano, your repertoire always attuned to the occasion and the guests who were present.

When I taste a favorite dish, hear an old-time song, or wear a sweater you left behind and see that it is a perfect fit, I know that you are near.

This book is an expression of unending devotion, admiration, and love.

I'll see you again.

Cast of Critters

Anty Annie

Baby Chick Chick

Belle Birdie

Bobalong Bird

Bumbler B

Flutter By

Franny Fish

Froggy

Fuzzy Chick Chick

Minnie O

Mr. Tree

Orchid

Rosie Flower

Squirrely

Sweetie B

Wiggly Worm

Woodsy

A Leap of Faith

Through a leap of faith, Froggy imagines a day when this wart will be gone, gone, gone.

One particular day, Froggy finds a wart, a slight imperfection, an irritant. Through a leap of faith, Froggy imagines a day when this wart will be gone, gone, gone. After a little while, that day arrives.

Froggy's big, jeweled eyes open as he looks at his critter friends and sees that they, too, are free of whatever ails, annoys, or irritates them. Mr. Tree's branches are no longer bare but flourish with greenery. Franny Fish no longer swims lost and alone but wanders the waters in the company of her brilliant schoolmates. Woodsy's aching back now is limber when chipping away at Mr. Tree or flying to a neighboring arbor to visit Belle Birdie.

Froggy and his critter friends rejoice and wonder, "How do the warts in one's world fade and fall away? What is the nature of healing? How does wellness happen?"

They know healing and wellness when they feel it— laughing at Squirrely's awkward antics, watching Bumbler B and Sweetie B make honey, helping Belle Birdie build a nest, and partying at Rosie Flower's blooming. The occasions and opportunities to live fully abound.

Froggy and friends discover that in this world of plenty, everything needed to live well is right there. It's in the earth, it's in the waters, and it's in the air. It's everywhere.

They must simply look around.

Perfection

All is right in Froggy's perfect pond.

Leaping farther and farther. Hopping higher and higher. What fun. What joy.

There are so many wonderful landing spots when Froggy jumps from here to there. A slippery smooth rock, padded with green fluff, is perfect for sledding and sliding. A nice thick and clunky cedar log, outstretched across the stream, has groovy bark with interesting striations and texture. When Froggy leaps and lands on all fours, there's a firm grip. With tummy snugly nestled on the surface, Froggy stretches and hugs the solid, comfortable log. He is relaxed, secure, safe, and at peace.

From this wooded haven, Froggy takes a deep breath of fresh air. So fragrant. So light. So spicy. So sweet. Froggy spies the source of this scent. A dazzling beauty is growing from the curvature of the log. Minnie O, a remnant of Orchid who grows on the nearby land, floats around the pond with Froggy on the bark-clad log they share.

Refreshed by the cool, clear, moving waters, more wonders appear.

There's glistening Franny Fish, swimming splendidly by, along with those in her school, while bubbles bounce to the surface. They are reminders to Froggy and Minnie O that the water breathes with life.

Froggy, Minnie O, and Franny Fish hear the melodic chorus above. A song begins with a steady tweet, tweet, tweet from Bobalong Bird. In response, Belle Birdie chimes in. Woodsy picks and plucks, and chips and chews away on Mr. Tree. Ah, sweet sounds of music fill the air.

Minnie O responds to the symphony with a more fragrant scent and a more luxuriant bloom. Franny Fish and her schoolmates pick up their pace with more vim as they swim.

All is right in Froggy's perfect pond.

Light

This is a day of light, more light, and more light still.

When all is well and good in Froggy's world, there's a sense of light—light weight, light load, light mood, light head, and light heart.

Froggy stretches and straightens all fours and jumps higher and higher. As if on a springboard and weightless, Froggy goes up, up, up and gently lands on the lanky, long, lush, green grass growing from terra firma, swaying to and fro, right next to his watering hole.

With all the leaps and bounds, a hungry Froggy seeks nourishment. A teeny, tiny bug and a wayward ant are just enough to satisfy him and yet maintain a lithe Froggy physique.

During this particular day, Froggy feels especially playful. After all, today is the summer solstice and the sun rose early and will set late. This is a day of light, more light, and more light still. The hot sun with a powerful, strong beam feels so good drying Froggy's damp, soggy back.

While sunbathing, the thick, silky grass that tickles Froggy's toes, legs, and tummy makes him laugh, laugh some more, and laugh yet again.

"Croak, croak, croak. Ha, ha, ha. How my critter friends amuse me, day in and day out. Let me explain."

Laughter

The sound of laughter—music to the ears and a balm to the soul.

Leaping through the thicket, Froggy spies Wiggly Worm slithering by, feasting on some goodies in the cider-soaked soil.

"A diet of delicious debris, awash in the finest of beverages. Nothing but the best of food and drink for Wiggly Worm, my connoisseur friend." Froggy laughs, "Croak, croak. Ha, ha." He loves even his own jokes.

On his trek, Froggy meets Squirrely, ever wagging a massive tail, a sign to Froggy that this critter is a friend. "Hey there, Squirrely. How's life climbing on Mr. Tree's limbs? Any new tunes up there in Belle Birdie's bel...?" Before Froggy can spit out "belfry" to complete the question, Squirrely scurries away.

"That one has ants in his pants." Froggy chuckles his throaty "Croak, croak."

"Please watch your mouth," Anty Annie gently warns, with a twinkle in each of her many eyes.

Froggy looks up and spies a variegated butterfly winging through the air ahead, flying forward and backward, to one side and then to another. "How graceful. How elegant. I'll call her Flutter By."

Froggy lets out another "Croak, croak. Ha, ha."

Flutter By's flip-flopping, flapping wings carry Froggy's belly laugh to critters near and far.

What fun. What joy. How good it is to hear the critters croak, giggle, ribbit, and guffaw. How good it is to hear your friends laugh, even when you are the *butt of their jokes* or, as Froggy likes to say, *the butter atop their corn.*

How wonderful for all to laugh in concert—the croak-croak from Froggy's bassooning belly, the hums and buzzes of Bumbler B and Sweetie B, the warbles and whistles of Belle Birdie and Bobalong Bird, the giggles and gurgles of Franny Fish, and the pips and pops of Fuzzy Chick Chick.

The sound of laughter—music to the ears and a balm to the soul.

Honey

They ply their craft, building a sweet honeycomb with many bee-sized apartments to store this gooey gulp of goodness.

Rosie Flower, Minnie O, Orchid, and many of their petaled friends welcome Bumbler B, Sweetie B, and others from the bee colony who are buzzing from flower to flower.

Dripping pollen from one flower and sipping nectar from another, the bees work away, creating new blooming beauties and, at the same time, collecting nectar to take home.

Bumbler B and Sweetie B transport as much nectar as they can carry to the workers in the hive and then return to the flowers again and again for more and more nectar.

With this bounty, the busy worker bees make lots of pots of honey. Pouring, molding, and shaping, they ply their craft, building a sweet honeycomb with many bee-sized apartments to store this gooey gulp of goodness.

"Just look at the luscious flowers that our colony contributes to the earth," Bumbler B whispers to Sweetie B.

"Yes," Sweetie B replies, "and listen to the lip-smacking yum-yums when our friends feast on the honey that our worker bees make."

How sweet it is to be busy bees and do such bee-autiful work.

Work

They work in unison with each ant and each unit playing a key role in keeping the colony safe and sound.

"We shall not be outdone by our bee cousins, Bumbler B and Sweetie B, and their hive of busy bees," Anty Annie counsels her kin as they perform their many antsy antics.

She orchestrates the working units of many, many tiny ants. One unit builds hills and dales. Another farms fungus for food. A unit of caregivers distributes antibiotics to keep the colony healthy. Yet another unit soldiers on, protecting the colony from a heavy foot.

The ants in Anty Annie's colony more than carry their weight. They work in unison with each ant and each unit playing a key role in keeping the colony safe and sound.

Anty Annie's scent perfumes her path, signaling to the surrounding ants, "Over here. Come this way. Mr. Tree has shed many, many leaves we can carry home to enlarge our nest."

A transport unit sniffs and follows Anty Annie's scent to the goods.

The ants learn that working together as one lightens the work load for all. What wonders a colony, community, or collective can achieve.

Sustenance

Sustenance from nature's pantry—
so good and so plentiful.

As Froggy wanders, the fullness, lushness, and richness of the earth become apparent.

Nice, nourishing crops in abundance sprout from the ground. Colorful fruits hang from vines and branches. Even the sunshine and air are there to provide sustenance.

"I'm here for you," the crops, the fruits, the sunshine, and the air seem to say.

Froggy is not imagining it.

The nutty ones call to those who can hear, "Over here. We're over here on the ground, in the forest of big chestnut, oak, and pecan trees. We have hard shells with tasty delicacies safe inside, just for you."

Woodsy, Belle Birdie, and Bobalong Bird fly over with some of their feathered friends. With their beaks, they crack open the shells and munch away. "So good. So, so good." Tummies full, the flock flies away.

Then Squirrely scurries over, puffs his cheeks chock full of nuts, and hightails home to share them with his kin.

Mr. Tree calls, "Come over here. Help clean up this place. The soil below contains rich goodies that are well past their prime. They are yours for the taking."

Wiggly Worm and other earth-crawlers feast on the leaves, roots, and nutrients in the soil. So doing, they make the earth richer and riper, very much appreciated by the flowers that grow nearby.

The tree sap shouts, "I'm so syrupy sweet. Drink up and enjoy a nice treat." Flutter By heeds the call and flies over with her dapper, flapper friends. They sip some sap. So sweet. So delicious.

Minnie O, Orchid, Rosie Flower, and their blooming buddies call, "Over here. There's plenty of nectar and pollen to swallow." Without hesitation, Bumbler B and Sweetie B buzz over.

Sustenance from nature's pantry—so good and so plentiful.

Parties

Let's eat. Let's drink. Let's sing. Let's dance. It's garden party time.

"Oh, how I love a party!" Froggy announces to his assorted friends. "It's time for me to leap along to the celebration honoring Rosie Flower's blooming."

From a seed to a bud to a lovely, red, fragrant rose, Rosie Flower takes her special place in the garden, along with the neighboring flowers that spring forth from the lush, green-covered ground, regaling colors galore.

"I'll see you when you get there," Froggy calls to his critter friends.

Creeping and crawling. Splishing and splashing. Wiggling and worming. Fluttering and flying. The critters travel to the garden party in their own special mode, moving at their own unique pace.

On Rosie Flower's special day, she takes center stage. "Hello, one and all. Thank you for visiting me here in full bloom, in the company of my many floral friends who color this glorious garden."

Rosie continues, "Look around at the blooming reds and pinks, violets and lilacs, fuchsias and magentas with, oh yes, the outstretched green leaves that open up to greet you."

"She has bloomed into pure loveliness," Belle Birdie tweets.

"So grown up, she is. Such a nice addition to this gorgeous garden," mumbles Bumbler B.

"She is splendid, our silky, scented, flowered friend," Flutter By adds as she flip-flaps her wings, spreading the rosy scent afar.

Rosie Flower continues her speech and stops when she sees and hears Froggy yawn.

"Enough of this sweet talk. Let's eat. Let's drink. Let's sing. Let's dance. It's garden party time," Froggy announces in his inimitable, throaty voice.

Rosie Flower concludes the talk, "Let the fun begin. Have a bloomin' good time. Oh, yes, and thank you for your many gifts."

Gifts

Gatherings. Gifts. The greatness of it all.

There are so many occasions to celebrate in Froggy's world of plenty. Rosie Flower's budding and blooming. Flutter By changing from a crawling caterpillar to a winged wonder. Mr. Tree growing from a seed to a sprout to a sapling. Franny Fish spawning the next generation of small fry. Froggy, too, becomes a cause célèbre when, as a froglet, he first departs the pond.

The critters acknowledge their friends' key rites of passage by offering presents, wrapped and ribboned. Yet, their true gifts are ever evident.

Froggy shares his "Croak, croak, croak. Ha, ha, ha." The sound of his laughter evokes joy in all.

Mama Orchid and young Minnie O freely offer fragrances, so light and so fresh. Their floral scent permeates the air.

Franny Fish simply swims, swims, and swims. Nimble. Steady. Determined.

She is on the go. She reaches her destination.

Bobalong Bird chirps and Belle Birdie responds. Back and forth, forth and back, the duo sing. Woodsy adds a steady thump, thump, thump. Each heartfelt beat bellows and beckons.

Bumbler B and Sweetie B, as busy as they are, make honey, ever sweetening the scene.

Never still, Squirrely jumps from one tree limb to another, chasing other kin. Happy. Active. Entertaining.

Gatherings. Gifts. The greatness of it all.

Toasts

His many critter friends lift a paw, flap a wing, toot a tune, and share a toast.

Today is Froggy's birthday. Now a not-so-tender age, Froggy is what you might call seasoned. But never mind. It's good to age and to do so gracefully. His many critter friends lift a paw, flap a wing, toot a tune, and share a toast.

With her sweet aroma permeating the air, Orchid speaks, "May the fresh, evergreen earth, caressed by the sky blues above, make your every breath heaven sent."

"Ditto," adds Minnie O.

In perpetual motion, Franny Fish blows some bubbles in Froggy's direction. "May you sparkle with every hop, skip, and jump you take. May you and may we take pleasure in the ebullience you exude."

Belle Birdie and Bobalong Bird dance and chirp, "May every do-re-mi you hear and every fa-so-la you sing create harmony that suits you to a ti."

Woodsy taps his message, "My dear, chipper friend, may you love a bushel and a peck, peck, peck."

Bumbler B and Sweetie B send a zinger to Froggy, "May you be zapped with honey and health, with sweetness and life."

Flutter By, who once upon a time could only crawl, flies by and throws Froggy a kiss, "May you be uplifted."

Fuzzy Chick Chick sheds her fluffy, downy feathers. "My dear Froggy, may your every landing be safe and sound and soft."

"May this earth nourish you," Wiggly Worm adds.

"May you reach the top of every hill you climb," Anty Annie toasts. "Always remember that friends like me are just a step away."

"You have sown well, my dear friend. May you reap rich rewards," adds Rosie Flower.

Froggy responds, "I'll drink to that and that and that."

Froggy is saturated in the roasty, toasty warmth of so many well-wishes from so many well-wishers.

Nests

How I admire you—a top-notch builder of a secure nest to hold eggs that will give way to your beautiful birdies.

Belle Birdie and her friend, Woodsy, occupy neighboring, sturdy limbs on a deeply and securely grounded Mr. Tree. Belle Birdie works away at building a nest, adding twigs, leaves, feathers, and pine needles stacked like oodles of noodles.

Woodsy is there, too, steadfastly chip, chip, chipping and chop, chop, chopping away.

"Help yourself to the many bits of bark," Woodsy offers. "I'm happy to make a contribution to the nest."

After more chipping and chopping, Woodsy pauses and asks, "How are those sweet babies doing? Any crackles? Any pokes? Any kicking of the shell?"

"In their own time and in their own way, they'll arrive. One of these days, in the midst of your chipping and chopping, simply listen and you will hear their chirps and chirrups."

Woodsy adds, "Belle Birdie, how I admire you—a top-notch builder of a secure nest to hold eggs that will give way to your beautiful birdies. May each babe be a chip off the old block. May your babies become you, my cherished, feathered friend."

Mr. Tree chimes in, "In tree talk, we say that the apple does not fall far from the tree. In other words, your babies will as wonderful as you are, Belle Birdie."

Belle Birdie, Bobalong Bird, and the many other birdies passing by tweet, warble, and whistle. Flutter By and friends flap their wings. Squirrely races from tree limb to tree limb with extra pep in his step.

Inside each shell that rests in the nest, the birdies yet to be born make a gentle sigh, a knowing sign that life outside of the shell will be warm and welcoming for birds of every feather. That includes the Chick Chick family living on the land at the foot of Mr. Tree.

Births

*This birth, like all births, is a
miracle.*

The shell wiggled, then crackled, then
broke as Baby Chick Chick came into
view.

This birth, like all births, is a miracle.
With a crack-crack here and a cluck-
cluck there, all of Baby Chick Chick's
family and friends rejoice. Fuzzy Chick
Chick, Papa Chick Chick, and many
other Chick Chicks are in awe of this
new creation.

Froggy, Orchid, Minnie O, Rosie Flower,
and Squirrely. Belle Birdie and Woodsy.
Wiggly Worm, too. All simply stop. On
the ground, in the trees, in the air, and
in and near the pond, the critters are
transfixed watching the birth and the
antics of the other Chick Chicks, along
with their fowlish kin.

The critters hear the cluck-clucks,
quack-quacks, moo-moos, baa-baas,
and neigh-neighs of other creatures.

Enchanted by the new birth and the
delight of those who gather to welcome
Baby Chick Chick, the critters are

quieter than usual. Froggy and friends feel close to the cluckers and the surrounding quackers, mooers, baaers, and neighers, and they feel close to each other.

Squirrely remains quiet and still just long enough to give Froggy a knowing wink that conveys the sense of wonder that both experience in that moment.

Woodsy pauses from crunching on a favorite Mr. Tree trunk. He looks down to witness the earth's critters below. He then looks up, dances a little two-step, and turns to see Belle Birdie spinning a pirouette. Woodsy nods to Belle Birdie. Belle Birdie nods back.

Together, the critters experience the wonder of this day.

Wash Day

On wash day, every thirst is quenched in the environs of Froggy's pond.

Froggy leaps from his log into the deep, wet, clean, fresh pond. In go his feet, his tummy, his back, his face, and his body. He lets the waters soak deep into every pore and soothe an ache here and a twinge there that come from his many leaps and bounds. The water that he absorbs in his drinking patch feels so, so good.

Froggy has company in his pond. Franny Fish and her school are swimming below the surface. Washed by the waters, their skin, their eyes, and their very beings are nourished as they travel this way and that way, meeting other schools of fish, large and small, that move through the purifying waters.

A ripple pulses through the pond. Some thirsty birds have landed. Bobalong Bird, Belle Birdie, and Woodsy take big gulps and drink away. With their innards washed, they splish and splash on the water's surface, bathing, fluffing, and primping their feathers. Satisfied, they burst into song and fly back home.

Back on shore, other critters—sopranos, baritones, tenors, and basses—bellow in harmony, singing a rip-roaring and rousing hallelujah chorus.

Mr. Tree and his arbored friends, along with Rosie Flower and her floral friends, have their wash day when the waters rain from the skies. Their leaves are made silky and shiny. Their roots are moistened from the hydrated earth.

On wash day, every thirst is quenched in the environs of Froggy's pond.

Hobbies

A hobby makes one limber, lively, and lovely.

All the critters have hobbies, activities that bring them pleasure and joy.

Some of the hobbies are physical. Anty Annie, believe it or not, is into body building. She positions each limb, assumes a perfect posture, and poses.

Bumbler B and Sweetie B often listen to the birdsongs around them, and they whirl and twirl and dance, dance, dance.

Flutter By is crafty, indeed. She loves fabrics, textures, and colors, and sews and knits caps, capes, and other wearable art.

Fuzzy Chick Chick loves teaching Baby Chick Chick how to decorate egg shells with squares and diamonds, dots and lines, and curls and swirls.

Mama Orchid and daughter Minnie O collect and categorize. They have samples of every type of orchid around. They can identify even the minutest details of their pedigree.

Mr. Tree is deeply into genealogy. He meticulously observes the roots and scrupulously studies the origins of his many critter friends.

Woodsy's hobby is akin to his day job of nonstop chipping and chopping. For fun, he crafts chunks of wood and chips of bark into critter statues to decorate the terrain.

Squirrely often traverses the ground, aiming for a hole in one. He kicks an acorn, a chestnut, or a pecan into a far-off hiding place. Oh, how Squirrely, the golfer, relishes this game.

And Froggy? This orator makes the most mundane, minuscule moment into a special occasion in which to puff and pontificate from his platform, a lily pad in his pond.

True to form, Froggy has a few words for his critter friends. "A hobby makes one limber, lively, and lovely."

All the critters nodded in agreement.

Fun and Games

*Treasure Hunt, it is, since it can
be such fun, fun, fun for every one,
one, one.*

"Let's play a game."

"What shall we play?"

"Name That Tune," suggest the birds.
"We know so many, many songs."

"Tag, You're It," propose the butterflies
and the bees. "We move so, so fast."

"Hopscotch," offers Froggy. "I can hop,
skip, and jump from square to square."

"Hide and Go Seek," adds Wiggly Worm.
"I can simply slither underground."

"How about Treasure Hunt?" suggest
the flowers. "Our roots lead the way to a
panoply of earthly gems."

"Talking about roots," notes Mr. Tree,
"mine stretch very far, very wide, and
very deep into a trove of tantalizing
treats."

"I love the idea of Treasure Hunt."

"Me, too."

"Me, three."

"Done. Treasure Hunt it is, since it can be such fun, fun, fun for every one, one, one."

"We'll divide into two teams. Each team will make a list of treasures."

"Yes, and each team will search for the other team's treasures. That way, we are both list makers and treasure seekers."

And so the game began.

Organizing into two teams, each critter sounded off.

"One." "Two."

"One." "Two."

"One." "Two."

The Ones, known as the Once Upon a Thyme team, gathered in the garden and busily made a list of treasures.

The Twos, known as the Two Timers team, camped on a comfy branch on Mr. Tree and chipped away, making their list of treasures.

With the sun high in the sky, the Once Upon a Thymes and the Two Timers completed their lists.

On behalf of the Once Upon a Thymes, Anty Annie said, "Two Timers, we want you to bring us a petal, a pinecone, a chestnut, a speckled egg, and some tasty maple sap."

Bobalong Bird, representing the Two Timers, requested of the Once Upon a Thymes, "Please show us a feather, an underground tunnel, a floating lily pad, a nest, and some sweet applesauce."

And so the hunt began.

Froggy could hear the critters hem and haw, buzz and saw, and chatter and chirp as they searched for the treasures.

With the sun a tad lower in the sky, the Two Timers returned with every one of the treasured items in tow. The Once Upon a Thymes showed the way to each of the treasures they hunted and found.

"We won," announced the Once Upon a Thymes. "We won, too," added the Two Timers. And both teams were correct.

"What do we do with the treasures?" they asked. "We already have so, so much."

A voice from the crowd of critters shouted, "We can afford to be generous. Let's simply give these treasures away." The critters voiced their suggestions.

"Let's give the pinecone to Woodsy's woodworking friends. They can use it when crafting their critter statues."

"Good idea. I bet the speckled egg will come in handy for the egg decorating class that the Chick Chicks attend."

"Let's give Belle and the other Birdies the feather to add to their nest."

"I hear that there's a fashion show approaching. Let's donate the maple sap and applesauce to the refreshments committee."

The critters found a home for each of the collected treasures. Thus, the list makers, the treasure seekers, and the recipients of the treasures became winners all.

Such fun, fun, fun, for every one, one, one.

Fashion Show

*Our fashion show will have so, so
much to chew on.*

Froggy greets his friends, "Rosie Flower,
I perk up whenever I see you clad in
your roaring, riveting red. Orchid, the
pearly pink and sky blue become you so.
I feel zen-sational when I'm with you,
my flourishing, floral friends." Froggy
can almost taste a peachy, perfect day.

"Look, here comes Bumbler B, all
decked out in a yellow jacket and black
tie. He is so dapper," says a smiling
Rosie Flower.

"Bumbler B, you're looking fine today,"
Orchid offers.

"Ditto, ladies," mumbles Bumbler B.
"We critters clean up nicely if I do say
so."

"Yes, we do, my dear Bumbler B. All this
sweet talk, first from Froggy and then
from you, gives me an idea. Let's have a
fashion show," suggests Orchid.

"I agree," adds Rosie Flower.

"I'm in," flirts Flutter By. "My flapping
friends love to show off the newest

trends. They'll be delighted to fly over to the guests to give a close-up look of their caps and capes of many colors."

"I'll get Sweetie B to parade her honey-colored fur coat," offers Bumbler B. "In fact, I'll start the buzz right now. I'll mumble that everyone is invited to strut their stuff, showing off their finest duds."

"I'll serve as the master of ceremonies," croaks Froggy.

"We'll provide a medley of melodious music," Bobalong Bird and Belle Birdie chime in.

"No need to worry about refreshments. I have a sumptuous stash of tempting treats to serve," offers Squirrely.

Mr. Tree interjects, "I'm sure that my neighbors can drop off an abundance of chestnuts, acorns, pecans, and cashews. My fruited friends can contribute apples and pears, and I'll ask the berried shrubs to shed their wild blues and raspy reds."

"Wiggly Worm and I will handle the cleanup," adds Anty Annie.

Our fashion show will have so, so much to chew on.

The fashion show began atop the knolls near Froggy's pond, a sacred place where the open skies, the waters, and the earth meet in friendship.

Froggy's big, beautiful, bulging, wide-awake, jewel-colored eyes have a panoramic view of the entire scene as he announces the models.

"Imbibe the fragrance and see the beauty of our flowered friends. Orchid is wearing a thin, green sheath topped with a colorful cap. Her lovely daughter, Minnie O, is wrapped in pastels. Rosie Flower is clad in a lush, red-petaled hat that opens wide to welcome the day."

"Notice the bees buzzing by. Bumbler B, modeling his finest yellow jacket and black tie, is escorting the stunning Sweetie B, fashioned in a fluffy, fleecy, flowing, fur coat with an extraordinary jeweled pin."

Every now and then, Froggy leaps to a rock in his pond, so that Franny Fish, along with her classy schoolmates, can hear the vivid descriptions.

"Look up and see our flying friends, winged in their caped creations of reds and blacks, yellows and oranges, and blues and greens. The colors, designs, and delicate fabrics make quite an impression."

Franny Fish, her surrounding floundering friends, and some big-mouthed bass flap their fins, make waves, and stir up a storm of applause.

As the day unfolds, it becomes clear from the smiles, laughter, conversation, and good cheer that the critters' fashion show is swimmingly successful.

The audience gives a standing ovation. The master of ceremonies, models, caterers, and cleanup crew all take a bow.

Froggy summarizes, "We had a wonderful day. Let us thank our lucky stars."

Leaders

Representatives of the many critter communities gather to elect their leaders, the Critters in Charge.

The critters acknowledge the land, water, and skies that lie beyond their patch of paradise. As part of this greater whole, they are aware that other critters affect their lives—the destiny of the nourishment burrowed deep and saved for a hungry day, the health and safety of the wooded homes where their kinfolk live and love and nest, the richness of the earth that sustains them, the refreshing air they breathe, the lifting of the fog, and the dispersion of the smog.

Every now and then, representatives of the many critter communities gather to elect their leaders, the Critters in Charge. Now is the time to decide, the time to cast a vote. What to do? What to do? What to do?

So much hemming and hawing, so much croaking and clucking, and so much mooing and neighing have occurred over the course of several silly seasons. Now, at the start of a new season, a mere handful of contending critters remains.

Froggy tries to see the contenders as critters who will work for the good of all, knowing that the same sun shines on all.

Froggy asks his friends, "What have our current Critter in Chief and Assembly of Critters done for the community that lives in and around our pond?"

He listens to their answers. "When storms are brewing, they send in Critter Contingents to keep the waters at bay."

"When we are in flight, we follow the designated traffic patterns provided by our Critters in Charge, making our journeys safe from other travelers."

"Sometimes, the neighboring communities impinge on our ability to build our hives, burrow our tunnels, blossom into fragrant flowers, or chirp and be heard. Whether knowingly or unknowingly, they step on our toes, and we sometimes ruffle their feathers. A Critter in Chief, with an Assembly of Critters, can harmonize our efforts for the common critter good."

"Enough talk," said Froggy. "Tomorrow we vote."

Prayers

May our leaders heed our prayers
that all may live well and thrive
in this world of plenty.

With the votes cast and the winners announced, now is the time to pray that the elected Critter in Chief and Critters in Charge will work for the good of all.

Hear the critters' prayers for their new leaders.

"May their hearts be softened."

"May they lead with compassion and love for all."

"May they discern the wheat from the chaff, the good from the rest."

"May they harmonize discordant notes."

"May they recognize their foibles and admit and correct their mistakes."

"May they be healed of their warts."

"May they repair the broken, release the injured, and lift all pain."

"May they do no harm."

"May their backward steps be short and brief and their forward leaps long and lasting."

"May they be mindful of a universe that knows no bounds."

As is often the case, Froggy adds the last few words, "May our leaders heed our prayers that all may live well and thrive in this world of plenty."

All nodded an "Amen."

Supermoon

Looking at the supermoon, the
critters quietly and softly sing,
"I'll be looking at the moon, but
I'll be seeing you."

On this night, all is quiet. All is peaceful. Time to rest. Time to sleep. Tonight, the moon is neither a sliver nor a crescent, neither a quarter nor a half.

This night, this gentle night, the moon is round, full, and big. This supermoon that illuminates the sky above has never appeared before, at least not during a critter's lifetime.

Those with eyes to see watch the moon so perfect, so magical, so close. They wonder about this glowing ball that inspires dreamy reflections.

Looking at the supermoon, the critters quietly and softly sing, "I'll be looking at the moon, but I'll be seeing you." Rosie Flower sees the face of her Superma who made music, music, music that delighted all. Looking up, up, up at the moon above, she hears Superma making more music still.

Superdad is with her, whistling away. Supergrandpa is there, too, lovingly listening.

In the moon that now seems so very near, the critters see many joyful, radiant faces of those who have passed on and live elsewhere now, in a far-off place that is beyond a critter's understanding.

Rosie Flower thanks the moon for shining so big and so bright. "I'll see you in the morning, moon dear. For now, sweet dreams and good night."

Renewal

The time, the moment, and the space are ripe for relaxation, rest, and renewal.

The winter solstice approaches. With the shortening of sunlit days and the lengthening of starry, darkened nights, Froggy and friends sleep in a bit longer and eat a morsel less. Foraging for food becomes more work with ice and snow atop the hardened ground.

Woodsy comments to Belle Birdie, "I chipped a nice winter home in Mr. Tree's trunk. There's room for you to take shelter. I have another safe, comfortable abode just around the bend on Trunk Turnpike."

"Thank you, Woodsy. I'll take extra good care of this hallowed, hollowed refuge from the winter's cold. On snowy days, let's unfold and flap our wings and visit Froggy on the pond. We will invite all the flocks wintering up North to join us there."

"The bird-bathing pond will be available to you any time," said Froggy. "Visit whenever you like and have a cool, refreshing drink on the rocks."

"I'll visit, too," adds Squirrely. "On a chilled day, I'll be sure to bring along my squirrely kids and my antsy kith and kin to skate on the glistening, gleaming, glowing, icy surface."

The critters know that in any season, in any weather, during hours of light and dark, the time, the moment, and the space are ripe for relaxation, rest, and renewal.

Praises

They praise the maker of the trees and give thanks for the chestnuts and acorns that nourish Squirrely, his family, and his friends.

Froggy hops from a log and plops into the water. "Oh, this living water is so cool, refreshing, and soothing. I will allow it to permeate my every pore. Hallelujah to the giver of water that hydrates and heals."

Scurrying up the mighty Mr. Tree trunk, Squirrely chases his many jittery, furry friends from limb to limb. Then down the trunk they all go, hover over a patch in the earth, dig a nice little hide-away, wag their bushy tails, and move on to another tree. Then up again, frolic some more, down again, dig again, and on and on they go in perpetual motion.

The squirrels and their many hungry friends stop long enough to gnaw at the shells and chew away. "Delicious. Yummy." With bellies full, they praise the maker of the trees and give thanks for the chestnuts and acorns that nourish Squirrely, his family, and his friends.

Flutter By flits among the flowers and marvels at the artistry, the dabbles, the daubles, the strokes of color, and the varied shapes. She stops to say hello to Orchid, now in full bloom, and visits Rosie Flower, wearing her finest red.

Flutter By is in her glory. "How lush. How lovely. This majestic garden is here for the pleasure of my fluttering friends, here to welcome us when we want to simply, gratefully rest, wrapped in the embrace of our folded wings."

Before flying away, she praises the gardener who grows the flowers that dot the earth with colors so vibrant and so bright.

Gratitude

In their world of plenty, the critters have so much for which to be grateful.

The critters express their gratitude.

"Thank you for the tunnels my kin build and traverse," starts Anty Annie.

"Thank you for each heart beat, beat, beat that keeps us in tune," adds Belle Birdie with a nod of agreement from Bobalong Bird.

Bumbler B continues, "I am grateful for the flowers that allow the bees to make the honey that sweetens this life."

Flutter By flickers by, noting, "I am thankful that this once creepy, crawling caterpillar was transformed into a winged wonder."

Baby Chick Chick expresses gratitude, "Thank you for my dear mama Fuzzy Chick Chick, my devoted papa, my sis, and my bro' for clucking in conversation and communion."

Franny Fish notes, "I am grateful for the schoolmates with whom I wander the waterways that are filled with fabulous fish and fauna."

"Thank you for the roots that ground me, this trunk that faithfully holds me upright, and outstretched branches that reach for the sun, the moon, and the stars," offers Mr. Tree.

Woodsy adds, "Thank you for the oaks, the maples, the elms, the willows, and all types of trees that stand tall as I chip, chip, chip away."

"I am thankful for claws that climb to great heights and a lithe body that goes out on a limb," states Squirrely.

Rosie Flower, Orchid, her daughter Minnie O, and their many floral friends acknowledge, "We are grateful for our ancestors who bequeathed an ancient wisdom and intelligence into our every cell."

Froggy has the last word, "My gratitude is for moving waters with floating logs and lily pads powered by winds that carry me to scenic sights that my eyes allow me to see."

In their world of plenty, the critters have so much for which to be grateful. They are truly blessed.

Signs

*Though I sometimes hide, seek and
you shall find me.*

During the fashion show, a cardinal
wrapped in royal red with black trim
landed on Mr. Tree's outstretched
branch and watched the show quietly
and intently for a very long time. "Look.
See me. I am here."

While the treasure hunt was in progress,
the wind whistled and the leaves
rustled. "Listen. Hear me. I am near."

When skating on Froggy's pond, flecks
of ice shimmered here and glimmered
there. "Follow me. I am everywhere."

On wash day, big, white, fluffy clouds
danced to and fro. They could appear
Froggy shaped or Squirrely shaped or
any other shape. Ever changing, the
clouds hovered close, drifted far, and
disappeared. "Though I sometimes hide,
seek and you shall find me."

On the day of Rosie Flower's blooming
celebration, the bees buzzed, the birds
hummed, the squirrels jumped, and the
chicks pecked. As they moved, so did

their shadows. "I am with you, now and always."

In Froggy's world of plenty, the critters work together and play together. They care for one another. They have each other's back. And they have more.

A faithful, forever friend fills the air they breathe, pulsates the earth they trod, and flows through the waters that quench their every thirst. This friend is alive in a great beyond.

The signs of their friend are evident every day, in every way. The critters only need to stop, look, see, listen, and hear to know that their friend is also alive in a great within.

Salutes

The formation salutes the star-studded skies.

High above Froggy, Flutter By, and Belle Birdie and high above the yard, the garden, the trees, and the pond, a V-shaped flock of winged beauties moves gracefully through the open skies, facing forward and then pivoting downward.

The flock dips toward the earth, flies for some distance, and sees the wide expanse of treetops covered in leaves of green, ochre, copper, amber, crimson, rust, maroon, and burgundy.

On this day, the flock sees that Mr. Tree is colorfully dressed and takes center stage.

The flock hears the chirps and chirrups of Belle Birdie's babies as they join a spirited chorus and senses a crispness in the air. The roasty, toasty scent of chestnuts, oaks, and pecans hints at the season's harvest.

Looking down, the flock spies the pond bubbling with activity from Franny Fish and her school friends. A splish here and a splash there show signs that a carefree Froggy is leaping the lily pads— free of irritations, imperfections, and warts.

How sweet this life is.

As the flock heads upward, the formation salutes the star-studded skies, a tribute to the magnificence, majesty, and sacred splendor witnessed while in flight.

More Sweet Talk

This world of plenty is here for all, including you, you, and you.

Froggy has a few more words of sweet talk. "My good critter friends, keep the many, many words, words, words you have read, spoken, or heard close to you. Let them remind you that this world of plenty is here for all, including you, you, and you."

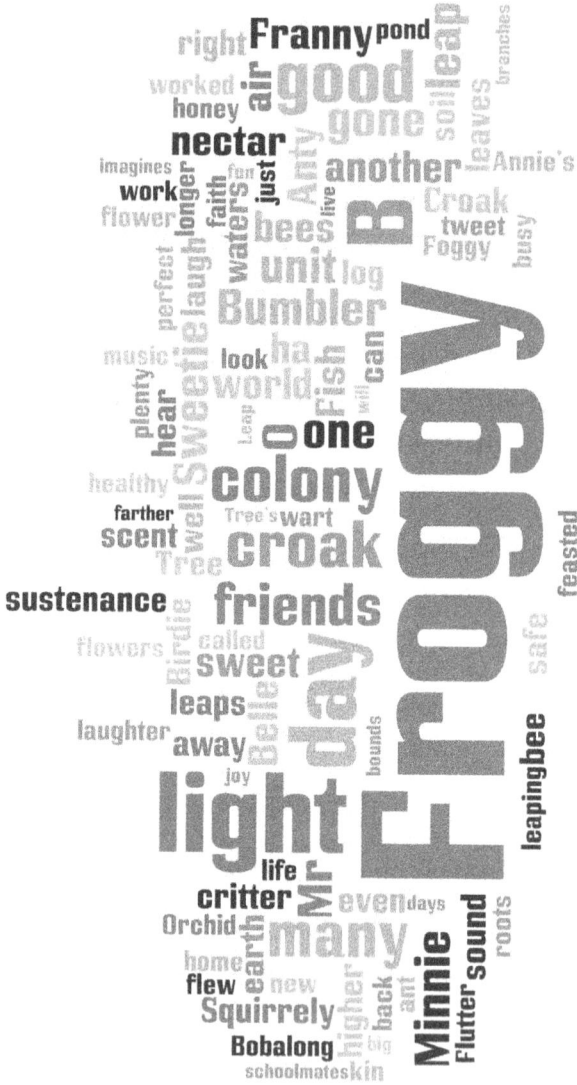

Reflections

A Leap of Faith

What does a life free from warts look and feel like?

Perfection

What do you see, hear, smell, taste, and touch in your perfect pond?

Light

What lightens your weight, load, mood, head, and heart?

Laughter

What corny jokes make you laugh?

Honey

What kind of sweet, bee-autiful work do you do?

Work

What does your colony achieve?

Sustenance

What sustenance from nature's pantry nourishes you?

Parties

How do you have a bloomin' good time?

Gifts

What gifts do you possess and share?

Toasts

What toasts do you offer yourself and others?

Nests

What are you doing to build a safe and secure nest?

Births

What wonders have you witnessed?

Wash Day

What thirsts does water quench for you?

Hobbies

What hobby makes you limber, lively, and lovely?

Fun and Games

In what games are there winners all?

Fashion Show

How do you strut your stuff in clothing and demeanor?

Leaders

What do leaders do for those who live in and around your pond?

Prayers

What is your prayer for leaders?

Supermoon

When you look at the moon, whom or what do you see?

Renewal

What space do you create that is ripe for relaxation, rest, and renewal?

Praises

How do you praise your gardener?

Gratitude

How do you express gratitude?

Signs

What signs indicate that you have a friend who has your back?

Salutes

How do you salute the sacred splendor in your world of plenty?

About the Author

Judith Ellison Shenouda is owner of Shenouda Associates Inc., a business that researches, writes, and edits the many professional publications that streamline processes, launch products, and promote each client's brand.

She has authored *Living Well in Froggy's World of Plenty: Sweet Talk to Read Aloud*; *Career Success in 12 Easy Steps: A Journal*; and *A Bisl of This, A Bisl of That: Eating Our Way*.

These books are available through online stores, including *Amazon.com*.

To learn more about the author, her business, and her books, visit her blog at *JudithShenouda.wordpress.com*.

To arrange a visit or a talk on a topic related to her business and books, email *Shenouda@easescommunication.com*.

www.ingramcontent.com/pod-product-compliance
Lightning Source LLC
Chambersburg PA
CBHW070937280326
41934CB00009B/1911